# Rope

# Rope

# Khairani Barokka

Nine
Arches
Press

**Rope**
**Khairani Barokka**

ISBN: 978-1-911027-23-2

First published October 2017 by:

**Nine Arches Press**
PO Box 6269
Rugby
CV21 9NL
United Kingdom

www.ninearchespress.com

Printed in the United Kingdom by Imprint Digital

Nine Arches Press is supported using public funding by the National Lottery through Arts Council England.

Supported using public funding by
**ARTS COUNCIL
ENGLAND**

*for my friend k.*

# CONTENTS

## *Ciek, Siji, Bloodbrushed*

## *Duo, Loro, Oil on water*

## *Tigo, Telu, Ink on palm*

*Ciek, Siji, Bloodbrushed*

# Pool

Stunt, little children,
seafoam light.

Backyard blues, splat
splutter.

Held breath so long,
crashwater in ears.
Friend's father scolds.
*I'd laughed.*

Any small child
next to any small child
is considered its friend.
*God, help.*

Hold breath again.

# climate nocturne

i sit on a man on the brink of love
and worry about the weather.
the bathroom light is on
and it will kill us. it will kill us
by virtue of contributing
to the whirlpool of heat
that will rise up and plunder
from the vast of wet soils,
will dry lakes of fishing,
lungs of cool air.
anxieties, insectlike,
swarming through the metropolis,
will cripple us slowly as we watch
our children drown, fry,
blizzards of fire
in the raging throat
of apocalypse.
           oh little boys, it is only 2017.

i remember: when the gross
weight of silence made way
for few vehicles in pondok indah,
when the area around the big new mall
(of three future malls) was still gross wetland
and sky, turned into a desolation of sales,
and now, now i see it, amidst shitty neon –
the tundra where he and i meet and our
memories never will, cracked universes
kept to myself, his own worlds
of past jaunts and homes, and how
we refuse to think of the future,

nor of the red past, a pact; is this
because it may be, may well be, that all
of our futures are parched –

i tire and bleed, dismount.
lie down in a nightscape studded with sirens, hear
        the metronomic hum of human breath.

## poem for r.

lightning strikes the sky,
skins clean air
for women.

shows earth's mantle:
no place
where purity lies
without danger,
cleaving,
a mouthful
of alarm,
feet gone to
thunderous
precipitate
in one dead blink,

at the drop
of a minor squall.

by the herb garden
breasts on a statue
dampen as its face
grits stone fangs
harder for protection.

horizon is droplets
of water now,
fool statue –
each ounce of
rainfall a woman.
each cloud a woman.

each ant trapped
in dirt's refuge
a woman.

nothing exists
that did not
escape from us,
didn't force us
to choose, quick,
what elements
soaked or dry
in forest and city,
desert and bedroom,
tundra and courthouse,
field and billow that
we as statue, raindrops,
insects, toenails,
vapour and lightning
wished to escape.

# Steel, Yourself

F train comes engorging
fist-first into the belly
of the stop like blood
from warm places,

dripped on the platform
and dried. Stoop, girl.
That's red you remember
and recognise from Friday.

You packed a jam sandwich
but won't get to eat it now.
Just a few metres down, and
you're holding breath solid,

suspended vision in a tunnel
of piss, no rain, no sunlight,

always three AM.

Mother's earrings you
leave behind on the dresser
in revised historical fantasy

rattling, instead, clickety-coo
under rodents' feet not so far from your
own persistent ankles.

# The Closing of the Bones

In the houses they live in afterwards, there is the ghost
of a framed shelter within the belly—one she'd laid pliantly
to rest, to set things aloft, first setting them alight. This spirit
rests with the olive oil on the kitchen counter, and sometimes
with the spinach and sambal, resting in the bowl painted hot
with red birch trees and coloured winds snaking double
round them. Air fed with exhalations, the pair carry the bowl
from rented vessel to rented vessel of their courtship made
solid, like the promise of freedom, like a child they knew
shouldn't want to be just yet, to live here now.

# conception

dogged speck
clot of blood
and all of us awkwardly
rivet-welding
selves to the earth
for another quiet week

i think eggs have self-awareness
i think they have a say
i think mum's said
no and no and maybe
and then she saw this one
little snake and sighed
and said

    "well. ok."

# Escort

*For JF*

Today, she tells you, her husband decimated a village
where ninety percent of the couples were truly in love.
He scattered their fidelity to the four winds and into
janitorial employment, the call girl's hair he smothers
in after the conference call a shade less ruddy than
hers was once. He notices.

If she asks you for your number, give her your
childhood best friend's secret. Give her the toys you
were never ashamed to play with, before you learned
how to masturbate. Give her your neon limbs.

See if she can remain liquor-stunned and platinum-
cocktailed when you kiss her like a child. Show her
the streetlights fading when the sun comes up, and
shame half-dries.

Everything she owns is a reflection. Bless you for
calling her beautiful.

# cutting

cropped short feels like exhalation:
a punk sigh of right.

something about long hair
reminds me of tears all down the front,

a friend after the first time,
before she cut it off to be strong
and then it happened again times two.

reminds me of tangled feminine juices,
guilt crystallizing down telephone lines,
after other friends cut their hair and
the forty-third man walks.

long hair
reminds me
of all my "her"s.
secrets of the majority,
walking open into
bitumen cities.

sometimes long hair
makes anger rise in tresses.
    mess. sinless.
    bless.

# Meteorology

**i.**

In summer,
I am your purple-and-soot,
my fingers in your mouth,
my ear against your supper plate.
Epidermis mixed
with creamed potatoes, Turkish bread.

I live here because you said
to storm in, briefly,
sans breathing cloud into
cracks in wooden beams.

I never weather anything
because I am told.

**ii.**

Hailstorm in the mouth,
crockery breaking
into repentance.

Coalfire temp,
a feather burning charred
against the grate
where we dry socks.

Your silence speaks fences,
also sky.

Parse this quiet for me when we fuck.
Lightning. I am a woman
unaccustomed to calm, so like
a sudden swallowing it is, cold snap.

This is how you pitch my winds
like tentpoles in the dirt.
"Hurricane yourself in one place,"
until I will.

Mathematical artistry,
make the arcs
of cosine, sine.
Precipitation tries
and fails to drop.

Loquaciousness thundering in other lives,
you become mute lover.

    With all this grasping soundless,

      are you saying "Thank you"?


**iii.**

Tangent:
gerimis is the Indonesian word
for light rainfall.
Sounds encapsulated:
grit, porridgey,
granular drops.

A sudden squall.


**iv.**

Galileo himself could not
predict weather by telescope.
You give me a brass miniature
that magnifies three times over.
The less soupy the fog,
the clearer.

Ave Marias make
bluebell-coloured echoes
from the church to the side.
In these skies,
silver linings desecrated
by pigeons.
Shits and giggles.

Our ideas
of what constitutes
extreme humidity split,
deep and opposed.
Too much, or
not nearly sufficient
for the required
warm trough of sweat.

Changes in the chill
like a metronome
to pacing, outpacing,
changes in the pulse.

Breathing so harshly
through our chests

that the rest of us is drought.


**v.**

Deluge.

# Epicdermis

It strikes me: the analogy of woman to country
recurs in part because, in fact, to some it's easy –
to visualise the gleam of the new as both
shore of the Indies (West, or as it were my East),
and a smooth stretch of sandy clavicle,
high-hilled buttock, fleshy ankle. Shining
shimmering splendid, Aladdin's new world,
all subcutaneous fat and follicles.
Colonise at will, with reliable prophylactics.

Wouldn't it be nice, if before the necessary culture clash,
they listened to the natives' oral wisdom,
became versed in the ethnomathematics
of the tribe, and read in the original tongue
the bafflingly complex philosophies of the gods,
in temples of perplexingly less savagery than presumed?

Baby, I'm just saying.

# To mess with the heart of a country boy

Shower his fruit stand in the city
with aches from long journeys –
you want a warmer highway.
You and Syaitan eat dirty rice
by the road – squat, with your claws –
and the road is stained with metropolis.

*Amen* go his churches and gong go
his withering temples, gone to the
steeples and dometops are aggregate
family members all his, watching your
sky-smitten skyscrapers fall.

There's a demolition you miss – like Mother's lullaby,
no longer yours, vast urbanity under chipped fingernails.
Yes: it's overheard street vendors, tiny alleyways,
all the soot-broken dreams in sparkle,
calling at your guilt from municipalities. So.

Push ring-fingering eyes away into the dirt
behind the old shed. Fly home.
Don't you bother to smooth a bent skirt
or to iron those tired pants for the journey.

Give the fallow pit of a nectarine
to his wide-eyed terrier, pawing
at the doors inside the house you are leaving
in the squalid afternoon with all its lights afire.

# Baleen July

Swallowed all four
of our lip-halves
gummy, built a whale
of a dungeon,
locked in rattlebone ribs
for old months and
silent letters sent petrified.

Nephews laugh outside
while the sun shines,
yawn during receptions.
We swordfight;
new grey hairs.

Mammalian jaws
disintegrate inchmeal.

Inside, krill pillows
where you sat go soft,
go too far apart.

Sleeping's relief,
night its masterfort:
a hum, a promise of sun,
like keeping a body
in the nook of a heart.

## Sea Turtle/Penyu

Salt-tongued priestess of the high seas,
   specimen-large, slow glide under leagues –

I see you feeling my shadow.
   Wet and small-faced,
      surface-snorkelled,

climbing breath down
       and across
    small rafters of waves.

Your archdome beneath the three Gilis,
   coagulating
      with white-person sweat
  and warm air,

I miss our quiet
     beneath all points of ocean.

Beat my heart ragged,
   knowing I'd left,
     when we were both meant for the blue.

# Wednesday's Child

Little captain of my womb,
she might have navigated the streams of becoming
with claws and iron, held on with alabaster nails
to the interstices of uterine walls.

Pirate queen, small interlocutor of necessary things,
my operatic diva of singing innards.
A *will I won't I become.*

Impossible as break-ins through barricaded armada,
as ocean captures of impenetrable raid ships.

In the blink of both eyes I did think her flesh
could become as tactile and wet
as fresh blood in saltwater, fish eyes in porridge,
your staying away was just as well;
ghost-child felt all mine.

May's sunshine-to-be emerging
from hips would have climbed to the bow of the ship.
Armed to the teeth with an animus of my making,
in a dress weft grey from marine winds, kelp,
crayfish shells culled from ominous straits,
and loved me, told you: *Get gone.*

# Stupor

McNulty was in my dream.
His wife was an Indonesian "tribal girl",
so said she – not his she,

the other she, the she who danced
in the bar, let him (McNulty)
touch her earring,
then was slapped,
repeated, again, by him, yes her in the car,

him from the front of it,
smacked with McNulty's white glove
(of course),
for calling his wife a tribal girl.

But his wife really was,
and a professor.

Even if she (professor she) hadn't been so,
why is all this a nightmare
to me (a she)
only upon awakening. What seeds
of swallowed god-king-mentality *girl* (my *she*,
myself) must have drunk –

to have it seem,
at first,
anything but.

# Lympha

Every way the water goes,
the light rushes across
its surface like a bolt of silk.
Closing my eyes,
I hear three women
whispering, *Swim up.*

All the birds can see
is the shimmer and jazz
on the plane of liquid,
pockmarked, frenetic.
Rabid light, and underneath,
not even the shadow of limbs.

I get self-conscious
and the river grit thickens.
Mouth stopping, shut
sealed by the current.

Underwater, the voices of three
strange-eyed sisters on the banks.

They see me plunge deep,
they slowly merge
into a single vocal rope.

Repetitive, distorted by the water, false clarity.
Lids shut, swirling in my seaweed hair,
as it pulses through and throughout.

This voice says,
*You run through the marrow of me.*
It says,
*I will haunt you for too many years.*

*Lympha: Roman deity of freshwater*

# Womb, REM

Fingers that smell like cacao
and melt in the sun.

Grabby with breathlessness,
slap of soles just run up a hill
for the woman in kebaya
who vends sticky rice cakes,
air punctuated with yells to stop.

He laughs as though placenta-wet,
as though Earth could not possibly be finite.

I wake and touch my lower belly,
*Not my navel you eat from, child.*
*Stay with me in dreams*
*and never come out.*

*Duo, Loro, Oil on water*

# The Writer in Exile at Teatime

In the city of asylum she waits with pears,
eaten with a spoon and written on the chin,
with each sloppy comma of juice.

She attaches, to each day, a mirage from home,
to be peeled from the illusory calendar
like a scoop of sweet stringy flesh from a fruit.

This was Sunday with the homes
like teeth in sepia;
Monday, brown dates between
forefinger and thumb.
Thursday's phantasmagoria:
the wooden mosque.

With a trickle of grey water like dredges
from Salsabila or distant settlements:
an old man she saw there once,
repeating ablution,
again, again.

# Bai Lan Bay

A small black curve on the map,
I think it will be shaped like the ghost of milk,
the bottom half of the nail of your forefinger.
Instead, curdled seaweed. Murky green,

blackened, with a battlefield of festering coral.
Rutted, grey, sand piercing the beatific sole.
An irritatingly assured thing,
a snail suckering on my thigh.

The sun is about to set; to appease you
I lie on your back in the water.
In fact, for almost five minutes.

I think of crawling molluscs,
and of the mould that has peeled itself
off of rock and seadust,
wrapped itself round the white band
of your swimming briefs.

You lay there calm as in chlorinated water,
all bodies of fluid the same to you.
You bear me on the small of you and
you are free. This is the ocean.

Our cleaving comes in steady
tomorrow, comes in certain, like waves.

# October/April

i.

Here momos are pinched into shape
for tourists who don't wash their hands.
Furrowed trenches into dough,
the colour of my mother's forehead
thinking of my hair beginning to grey
in a place with no islands like this –

*How will she survive outside of*
*saltwater surrounds, borders of coral?*
*Her toenails might shrivel*
*from the weight of travel,*
*the mauve exhalation of escape.*

The buried here believed in the wracked curse
of crossing seas, Jung Bahadur Rana almost doomed
to castelessness, traversing ocean in 1850.
They'd incinerate our hunters' maps,
hunch-strewn navigations, amorphous anniversaries
on bodies of water.

We pass by curious strangers with flashy eyes,
all parties' battle-axes sharpened by the sight
of shop windows splayed with Gurkha knives,
open-mouthed prayer flags run riot.
Desire is a transient thing,

quietly washing our skin
into the drains of Kathmandu.

**ii.**

After the quake, a friend there,
calm enough in time to say,
"Things are beginning to feel normal."
I burn with the extraneous shame
of someone who travelled in the haze of vistas,
in the homes of palpitating other bodies.

Who knows what this is like,
the stealing of a memory from all that is continuous,
bed and expected meals tomorrow, kin held inherent
as mountain to fault line, hearts in perpetuum,
frail life, spit blood, pained hoarse, precarious,
and prayed for by the singing bowl.
Survival is an eternal thing,

quietly washing its skins
into the drains of Kathmandu.

# Empathy for Cathedrals

*For EC*


We come here looking to stab down
mystery in the eye, pursue it to the cemetery end.

Venerable abbeys always still dying
a whole four centuries before the year
the Duomo is spent with its own construction,

pried from God's will first decreed
and into the twentieth century,
the year faith in stone is sighed out.

Ribcages enter the hollow en masse.
Candlelight on wrinkled moles.
The troubles crackling through the congregation,
piercing the leather of holy books,
letters scrubbed raw from the inside;

eau de camphor,
and all the Marys draped pale.
*Jesus has been black sometimes,*
*why not his mother?*

Observe glass stained with quiet,
and cracked palms on the seats,
and confession box.

From a childhood of Eids in fields,
and the courtyards of mosques,
I try to suck in this grown fear
of darkness cramped into rectangles,
of spiritual claustrophobia.
            Makes confessing difficult.

I prefer the heights
of ceilings over pews,
reminding us:
vacuity might breed awe.

# Tsunami Pilgrims

We seek out pain in lurid glimpses –
bent palm, shell from Lhok Nga,
where waves hit the treetops
and deluged the cement plant.

Near the leftward curve of the bay,
a marooned ship's chemical bullion
leaching out into the Indian.

*Do I sell these things in little jars?*
*Hone memories tongue-wrapped for relatives, repasts,*
*parsed words and round vowels,*
*tasting like rawness and saltwater?*

We wrap in plastic an oblong
displayed for the vendors
of foible as goodness,

and follow others' nightmares
here, to the sea.

# Flood Season, Jakarta

When the brown tongue of water
rises up to meet us here,
the house will be gone.
While inside the minds of islanders –
cushioned on the hills
of this sinking spectacle
of cardboard, blood, roads
twisting on each other like yarn
and neon, the flash
of a smile for the cameras,
journeys for food,
immune to eviction,
the rasping grey of the air –
we will be none.
Specks of paper floating
and mooring to the curb,
collecting under a tent
and against the grate.
While inside us,
we will never have felt
more present in the world
nor deadened, alive to the whims
of rivers and the sea, and bare.
Meaning bolts itself to hunger,
like the promise of fleshy
endless layers in a rice grain,
soft, half-fermenting, caught
under the folds of a nail.
Into our dreams, paddy fields

withered with drought or heavy
and drowned, will seep slowly
until soaked with them; pebbles and glass
under trucks rushing manic to the capital,
bringing and wresting, oil drums, men,
boxes of ginger candy, forests of logs,
chairs made of water hyacinths.

# Balada Gayung / Ballad of a Water Dipper

*For Yangti*

My father would tell me
how you'd edify bathing,
suggest the literal speaking
as acolyte to each arm and leg.
Stroking undulations of belly,
pouring gratitude through water
into flesh and femur.

Showers taught me nothing:

hit with the cold staccato sting of droplets,
I'd remember lying next to your throat
with its forgotten myths,

panic to place where I'd hidden your gift of a figurine,
a farmer boy playing a bamboo ring flute on an ox.
Totem for origin: a people of soilmen and flautists.

We never got to talking, my love,
about how much more humane it is
to bathe using dipper on limb by limb.

All this to say that this morning I took one to my body,
and remembered.

# Swimming

My father warned me not to enter waters in Vermont, but the landsmen had named the falls 'Journey's End'. Presumably, where illness too could wither and plunge to death.

In flight from a low-lying cliff of wet, the back of my skull escapes cracking by the length of a gasp. Ice throat of the river felt all through the weekend, when allies drive up from the wilds of New York and we play at fey exhilaration, women of the woods.

Cascade with an exceptional name. See how the crackling cold warms your marrow, while all is bursting in another way entirely, rained through the bone and only just beginning.

# Letter to a Miscarried Sister

I've been thinking of how to love someone
who was neither birthed nor weaned.

The arcane in the blood,
the imaginary in families,
how we conjure for ourselves
the ventricles of safety,
arteries of permanence,
succour in the face of another.
Clanning allegiance
from a clot of blood.

How we can tell
that someone has left,
or never departed;
if our grief has been buried,
or cleared from the pith.

If you are as mud-scraped
and vicious as I am,
it would be a comfort.
I see you winged, purple,
bloated, made of leaves,
cracked glass.
I have been less humble.

If you grant me salvation,
I will grant you respect.
This is a form of apology.
This is a form of want.

# Molly Schwartz and I Have the Same Legs

Perhaps there is a different way
in which geneticists, genealogists,
tailors and prostheticists
should now see the world,
now that we know Molly Schwartz
and I both have the honour
of legs shaped suchly.
Clearly there are differences
in pigmentation, nuances
of ankle and calf,
perhaps even veinage;
regardless,
on a couch in Brooklyn
there are notable similarities.
If we may say so, unusual instances
in which people comment
on chuckling God's bestowment to us
build character. Nay,
they allow us to chuckle back
at this God, and at people who assume us
strange by virtue of our limbs.
*Hark!* We say, *Lo, the various*
*specimens of man who have loved*
*these rather large calves.* Indeed,
we revel in their gossamer skin
and insouciant geometry. Truly,
no woman is an island.

# Temple of Literature, Hanoi

"Nothing is simple", says a man in his sleep.

Doubtful; many things less fussed with tangle: days before, five temple courtyards the light thrashed through, giving just myself joy. Corpus shaking with insect sounds, barraging violent in constant treetops.

No sin unforgiven by cicadas, cracked double with the weight of how *homo sapiens* break and chafe. All these terrors, storming bats, we split and split ourselves. Arthropods cackle plain.

Two schoolgirls tracing prayers on the red-painted wall with index fingers. Watch them speak to the gods, like thieves casing haze and cloudlets for some of that peace.

# Triptych

**i.**

Hymn:
Thank you, claws in muscle and bone, for tearing me whole to bring into being this naked, barefoot heart. This wild heart, slinging blood-ribbons slicing precision-thin; this gasping makes me whole, I am all-cells awake, my aorta to dirt, my limbs ground to pain and rising so many times, my breasts leak sky and phoenix-wing. Thank you abysses, rock-bottoms, cruel mind, false masters, morasses of salt – I am singing.

**ii.**

The anaerobic crumple begins again in quiet, in the dark, red habit. / You fold us in; eyes too open meaning *brave*. / Cracked paper, you and I. Miasma. / Origami and patience and breath.

**iii.**

Asymmetry's electrical thunderstorm – lightning splints the ribs, splits the fist, tempest's temper in the palm. Dawn.

# Secret

Under my navy-blue brassiere clasp
is a ball of lead-weight, white-hot dust.

Scorching, bucking, hidden by
painslaying buckets of pills
so small and pale in my ironed grasp.

When my love says, "You taken
your midday ones?", he is quietly
shouting. His calm voice,
silently grabbing my shoulders
to scream at me, "Please,
don't forget. What he hurls, he sends
so wide, to slit you inside out."

## Poetry to Self

Ingrate – I've caught your tongue in the dead of sleep,
soldered myself to your skin over nine lives,
played lone friend, lone adversary,

suffocating in synapses like a boiling pot,
the universe encrypted in my little finger –
you sucked on it on barren planets with unfamiliar names,
Mars Rovers colonising horizons.

When you were five and kind, I came smiling.
You vomited me puce onto shitty lines,
cringed me wholehearted.

Goddamn you,
the shit I've forgiven.

Funnyface, this arrogance and weakness
belong with each other in the dirt,
but I'll wait.

All your dead have been telling me
of their relief that still, fool woman
I nursed at the teat, you reach for my ankles,
hold tight.

# The length and breadth of space

To mark the ways of journey times with forefinger on a map.

To wipe blackened sweat off a father's brow, as he naps against the linings of a boat.

To snap your fingers when you read on your phone an article, a hopeful sign, another land's parliament, your fingersnap inciting the incensed cries of a nearby baby who despises travel.

To hoard war like lapping waves in your chest, to let it out in dreamscape, to wake in a clap of thunder with night terrors, speck of shore in the distance.

To cheat in a game of poker, smiling down into your lap, as a way to extend the enjoyment of having remembered to slither in getting your way.

To snag your flapping skirt on a piece of barbed wire, as you cross in a horde an unknown farmer's acreage.

To remember what it is to breathe with the calm of a stationary buoy – to have the time to think about the wheres of a someday-holiday, to make love not thinking of tomorrow.

To refuse all condescension against a search for refuge, to try to find the rapture in a daily cigarette.

To negotiate at night your flights of fantasy, living with ghosts trapped in amber. Spirits knowingly amidst everything your hands may hold in a day.

*Tigo, Telu, Ink on palm*

# Pineapple

Henceforth, Fruit may never stand for Woman as a matter of course, automatic simulacrum. Representing desiccation and death, its husk shrivels seeds, invariably consumed by the indiscriminate, pulped, ground, chopped. Tossed; force-fed syrup. This pineapple on the canvas may only be a woman when laid right, against an abstract background and cleaved by its self alone. Mane of forest, feral, fecund. Imposing, monolithic, millennia apart from the tales our grandmothers tell us of nanas' curse of vaginal ill-health when eaten, yet retaining *all the menace of such myth. A pox on you and your vaginas,* it could say – but it loves the pith of a woman, and would never strike fear in her heart, like the murder of armoured, segmented flesh, fork gone runny with sweet yellow juice.

# Chéf de cuisine

Braised artichoke. Lamb hearts tossed with a sprinkling of balsamic vinegar, but not without the special ingredient slashed over both meat and vegetable – a secret from childhood, invented in the kitchen where she first saw death, swallowed grief by eating the carcasses of living things until the weight of killing lessened, and life became pains and fatigue she had earned the right to from decades of sweat. Such liquid out of her pores from trying, a straight line through to glory without looking to left or right; loves thwarted, uterus protected from end-bringing life, all time sucked into a licked-clean plate, a greasy pot, presentation that reminded one enthusiastic diner of a Goya. Enough perspiration to refill the basins of prehistoric oceans, now deserts where patrons flew in to taste her wares, adding, she knew, with the fuel of those planes to the weight of the change that would render us extinct, where she remembered for only one minute now, each slab of day: the sweet blood of undercooked chicken on her tongue the night her mother had slipped with the knife.

# Dot

Darama's wooden-framed photograph:
Great-Grandmother could easily stay
her incandescence with a bindi,
notwithstanding choice of white mukena
for Subuh, Dzuhur, Ashar, Maghrib, Isya,
palms raised up and again (for contiguous
protection of children, eggs, rupiah,
the peace of knowing heaven is one's
own for the resting, after the world of
graves, Judgment Day, reliable reckoning).

On television, a blonde teenager is gyrating
to her own voice autotuned and repackaged,
the red dot just visible beneath her bangs.

Casting a gaze through the gallery, my eye
catches only the carousel of round, crimson
stickers, marks signifying exchange and value,
substitute for a sense of fullness. Perpetual
swirl with them, dizzy. Each piece they adhere
to is a woman of possible South Asian descent.
Picked apart in a vertical scan, by urbanites
whose quiet air tastes different from that
of washing and herbs, calming fears with
two sons and dzikir beads, a steady gaze in
monochrome, unflinching without a lover –

none of them my mother's grandmother.

# Ramadhan

Count on always more in the wings;
on incessant Jibril, flying down at eight
to stroke your thin cheek with feathers.

Tickling skin like you've heard
Satan teases rocks with fire.
Refuse to write the rhythms
of prayer in italics, it's not that exotic.
This is how you got raised
and woken too early:

hordes up-and-down with black
peci, white mukena, scarlet
post-dzikir sunrises, each year gone
with its month of dates in the mouth
when the dark bleeds in.
                            Television
blaring azan and inevitable local
waterfalls on-screen; Maghrib.

Four other junctures of daily worship,
a small spoon after,
            cool at the ready in sweets.

God betrays everyone fast –
one month must be taken
to try to forgive Her for it;
sing in quiet chanting together.

Take off your artifice, throng at the table,
solitude and quiet for every other time.

# Baffle Roof

The structure above the boy napping
on a frame, hammocked by cerulean
thread, wound round serpentine
and tied to its edges, is a roof.

The pastels used to coat windowed
barriers against the chill of Rajasthan's
November – another strain of roof.

The warm welcome of a woman,
thirty-two, into the folds of the
family she'd left for a husband
who, like the others, piles bricks
in Qatar and accidentally sends
her a picture of a woman with too
much kohl around dark eyes, allowing
her, finally, to kiss the man behind
the counter at the jewellery shop –
in broad daylight – causing consternation,
but somehow, reprieve; and in lieu of
tears, this unexpected returning to,
enveloping in, a deeper kind of love.

This, too, a roof.

# Rigour

This is what they will say about my daughter
and her eyes: that the way they haunt your
memories are vestiges of trauma, of how
a child was caught between battling tribes,
her reddened feet, chapped and just visible
beneath one ragged hemline, laid waste to
near-bleeding. *Girl, aged eight,* page 11.

It was her birthday. She was smiling again,
moments after the man left our village,
having been unsure of how to reconcile the
reach of zoom lenses with a robot cartoon
seen that morning – both unwieldy, pointing.
Washing off the ruddy paint we'd placed
by her room. The war had never touched
our subdistrict; all roads to it were closed by
3pm. Their jeep driver would never ring the
bureau chief. My daughter stood by the side
of the road, having drawn a rusty, laughing
rooster on paper with the balls of her heels.

# Rules of Engagement

Both sides must be steadfast,
teeth bared in politeness,
the minutiae of planning joy
in a ledger.

A well-worn painting
in the living room
of my grandparents' old house
standing watch;
two fisherfolk
of indeterminate gender,
sombre tones of workaday toil.

A prayer for women
who elope from Jawa to Malaysia
to nip Immigration's say
between two fingers,
for a few months
of watching your men
eating breakfasts of cooked rice,
ikan teri goreng.

Each handful sensible fuel
for breathing free
from the weight of papers,
spilled ink.

# Artist Statement

When I'd whittled the first miniature, he had left the night before. I'd felt violent, which is a human emotion, and this is how I'd channelled it, with the gouging of pockmarks on tiny kindling. Those elvish arcs at the tops of the ears, those were what his had looked like. I'd intended destruction, and, instead, created in his image.

Work in a stupor, then in a trance, then seemingly in dreams – my sleep disorder run riot, a dangerous secret to harbour from the intricate knifing of wood.

Everyone had tried to call the house, then had assumed me on another trip to the shore for supplies. When my brother knocked, I'd held my breath.

Fifteen figurines later: all of my loves in a row. I had lost my day job. It was time to ring a friend from school who'd begun to work at a gallery.

# Textile Display

Crisp to the fingers, the works in progress
are not the feltfall I'd assumed, allowing
a stranger to my left to veer towards *crestfallen;*
heat-seeker. We whisper what we know about
the artisan and later fall into each other,
monsoon-bound alchemy, inlays of shoes gone
clutchy to our soles with drizzle, mucky.
Pulse beet red, quickening to catch a lift.

Half-asleep, tiredness upsets the bowl of
my mouth to tell him a secret that explains why
I shuck off night terrors with warm milk,
expose more obvious distresses.

When I rouse to, he has pulled my hair up
and away from my neck on the pillow,
round the collarbone painted with my brush
and watercolours a mosaic of trees, framing
the dune below neck far down into canalillo,
and on the right swell of my belly, a tinamou.

Opened the windows to rain,
and gone to make sure
the memory presses in cellular,
flattens, dries as slow as the
wet season, toughens into skin.

# Ragging

It was difficult to know which cloth to suffocate the wall of his memory with: pinstripe shirt in carnevale colours, sweater with the insignia of an unnecessary bar bingo team.

He'd wanted the kitchen painted blood orange, noting the exact shade of pulse that flurried to her lip when she bit it.

Biting in it, dipped in smart smokey tones, his socks, all fifteen left in the drawers, mismatched and crumpled, doused with her hands in buckets of pigment, applied to every surface that threatened to amount to trigger.

The act, *a conscious thought,* like larvicide.

She could never sell the house otherwise, in case another woman was prone to biting the outside of her mouth when inflamed, driven to pressure on the skin, the changing of one's own tautness, reddened cries gone to the ends of all rope.

# Sakinah

Where was Malin Kundang when you needed him,
for commiseration? Humans turned mineral artefacts
prove difficult to come by around the Melacca Strait.
You stand lofty in sun, jungle clearing: yellow, pale
daffodil where the light catches what would have
been your shin, your knee, visitors craned up at
the curves of your now-multiplied necklines during
events, obliviously snapping photographs, ears
silent to blatant screams. In time, you stopped trying
to be heard. What was your supposed sin? Vanity?
Lust? Bloodlust, a fetus inside you couldn't bear
to hold? Were you too beautiful to have been truthful,
too trusting to imagine being a sculpture for the rest
of your days? They never tell us that Malin Kundang
had tried to reach his mother, many times. It was she
who first turned him away. In the night, frogs croak by
your ankles; you hum a song for petrified aluminum.

*Malin Kundang is a Minang folktale about an ungrateful son, who
returns from making his fortune and shuns his mother. As punishment,
she turns him to stone. Sakinah is the title of a sculpture by Ahmad
Osni Peii in Rimbun Dahan Arts Centre, Malaysia.*

# Fresco

The Sistine Chapel, where the
two cupped palms of their Lord
take in this: two men melding
twinned lips to rejoice at milder
climates, in ascendancy to an
earned salvation. Tell me Saint
Peter wouldn't have looked at
Michelangelo and marvelled
at subterfuge, strength, desires
made immortal on a wall caked
with the sweat molecules of
slow-footed tourists rising high,
meeting the men where they've
already soared to the ecstasy of
just being up, flown, hardening.

# Large Canvas

*For Tran Dan, who enjoys frightening fellow artists*


You are calm that these woods lack safety.
Silver motifs and swaying cats; where are
the parents? Human children easily sway
themselves into the path where eyes are
devoured by what's been brushstroked up
in the leaves. While you wait for each layer
to dry, tree spirits crawl thick into painted
globules. Such representation is alchemy;
cursed potions too run chemical. Take two
parts of advice with you in archipelagic old
growth. One: my father taught us to speak,
upon entering a new, hilly forest, alone,
an offering of Assalamu'alaikum. Peace be
for the fanged ones Allah might set upon us.

A second warning: repeat this when you lock
up the studio for the night. There are ghosts
for whom a gentle salutation might balm
an urge to escape the cut of stretched-out flax,
to pull to the world you've created the crux
of all your fears. Lustrate the oils with voice.

## Luminous Silver #9

Gargantuan tombstones,
Taj Mahal, mausoleums,
while under our feet
lovers buried their
half-will to live,
>           feeding grandchildren
>           with aubergines
>           nourished from
>           disintegrated bone.

At Yangti's funeral,
an uncle says
to four of us cousins
clustered in a row,
"Why do you artists
always wear black?"

So soon,
her permission for us to laugh.

# Sungai Di Pesisir / River on the Shore

Ada sungai di pesisir.
Sini kalian.
Ikat tali diri ke samudra.


/


There's a river on the shore.
Come closer.
Tie the rope of yourself to the sea.

# Rope

Enter this room
with something to unknot,

each sinew a crumple
of nine thousand braids.

Pelicans crowd the bay;
outside is a storm of

*fester, hungry,* fish
in wide bowls of mouths.

The darkness in this room
is a full berth for fear

to clutch its flayed hold on.
Step here, cracking your cries

of expectations gone grizzled,
rest your wet head

in the nook of the door.
Watch me cut through

a minotaur, head lolling
down in my arms. Soft beast.

This is not a gift for any stranger.
This murder was to strangle Myth

whole in the cranny of the maze.
A beast in your chest, choking,

and no stories now from the dead.
I want you to see how both of us

make Time go from the present.
Everything in these four walls

an action, a slitting. Watch –
fire ants crawl to the horns.

# Author's Note

Regarding the section titles, the first two words of each are Baso Minang and Javanese for "one", then for "two", then for "three". "Ciek" and "siji" mean "one" in Baso Minang and Javanese, respectively, "duo" and "loro" mean "two" in each of those languages, and "tigo" and "telu" are "three" in them. Being half-Minang and half-Javanese, it strengthens me to include these languages in some small way in this book.

## Additional notes on language:

**1.** In 'Dot', mukena refers to the loose covering over the head and body that Indonesian Muslim women wear to pray, usually white (but also available in all kinds of colours). Subuh, Dzuhur, Ashar, Maghrib, and Isya are the names of the five daily prayers in Islam. Dzikir is the repetition of religious words, including the names of God and holy phrases.

**2.** In 'Ramadhan', see (1) for mukena, dzikir, and Maghrib. Jibril is the angel Gabriel. Azan is the call to prayer.

**3.** In 'Rules of Engagement', ikan teri goreng is fried anchovies.

**4.** Re: 'Cutting', Alaina Leary of *Doll Hospital Magazine* wrote a nuanced article for Racked, entitled 'Haircuts Are a Shorthand for Trauma on Television' (May 22, 2017). She discusses hair cutting as both a legitimate way in which some women deal with trauma/misogyny, and an act which should not be taken as an automatic stand-in for coping with trauma, at the expense of recognising other symptoms and urgent needs.

# Visual description of cover

The cover of this book is 'Life, Agonda Beach', a photograph I took in 2013 of five wild horses running in a circle on Agonda Beach in Goa, under cloudy skies. Three are dark brown, and two are whitish grey. On the edge of the sea to the right, behind the horses, is a stone formation made of two boulders, one flat and wide, one stouter and smaller. The water is calm, waves are lapping. There is a logo for Nine Arches Press.

# Acknowledgements

Thank you to my editor and publisher Jane Commane of Nine Arches Press for helping to realise a longstanding pursuit, as the midwife to this book, and a pleasure to work with. Thank you to my poetry colleagues along the way who have transcribed life in vocal and written form and given me courage, and every event organiser who's treated poetry and poets' bodies with care. Innumerable people should be thanked here who have fed these pages, perhaps without knowing so; I thank most of all my patient, encouraging and generous-hearted loved ones: family members and friends, caregivers and health providers, and guiding lights living and in another spiritual realm, from Widji Thukul to Frida Kahlo, to my grandparents Soekotjo Sastrosoekotjo, Sri Martini Sastrosoekotjo, Ramli Hadi and Sayang Syarif. This book is for you also, for being with me until it became.

My thanks to the editors of the following publications, in which versions of some poems in this book have appeared: *Banana Writers, Cha: An Asian Literary Journal, Datableed, ISKRA: A Poetry Anthology, Jaggery Literary Journal, Junoesq, The Long White Thread of Words: Poems for John Berger, Magdalene, Media Diversified, Murmur House, Poetry Review, Rambutan Literary Journal, Rogue Agent Journal, Sin Fronteras/Writers Without Borders, Stairs and Whispers: D/deaf and Disabled Poets Write Back* (co-edited by Sandra Alland, Daniel Sluman and myself), *Surabaya Beat, tender, Tongue, Transom, Truthdig,* and *Wordgathering*. In addition, a few pieces were first published as/in paintings, at the Rimbun Dahan Residency group show "Bricolage" in 2015. "Luminous Silver #9" is taken from the title of a painting by Wong Perng Fey.

Work on this book was completed in many locations, over ten years; to read this manuscript again is to sheaf through a map spanning Asia, Australia, Europe, and the Americas. Often ill-equipped in my travels, I thank my kind hosts, grant-givers, and residencies, among others Rimbun Dahan Residency in Kuang, Malaysia; the women of Bori Village and Sandarbh Equilibrium Residency in Banswara District, Rajasthan, India; the beautiful Village Video Festival at Jatiwangi Art Factory, Jatiwangi, Indonesia; and Vermont Studio Center in Johnson, VT, USA, this last place where I would definitively reembrace *poet* and *artist* as states of being in difficult times, as not frivolous but fundamentally important, if we are to try to survive and to support each other. I also thank the various other institutions that allowed me to be where I was when writing these poems, as well as my wonderful students, and my teachers, Wanda Hagedorn, Barbara Ganley and Hilda Llorens, and including dearly departed friends Om Ben Anderson, Pak Bronto, and Ibu Anggani.

Finally, thank you to you as an individual reader. I hope *Rope* ties something to you that is felt, and would love to know if so. There is always more to cling to, to unknot.